D1151100

Free Run

by Stephen Rickard

Published by Ransom Publishing Ltd.
51 Southgate Street, Winchester, Hampshire SO23 9EH
www.ransom.co.uk

ISBN   978 184167 470 4

First published in 2010

Photograph pages 4/5 - copyright © 2008 Thorsten Rust; all other photographs copyright © 2009 Andy Day kiell.com.
Many thanks to Dan Edwardes and Kiell for all their help.

A CIP catalogue record of this book is available from the British Library.

The right of Stephen Rickard to be identified as the author of this Work has been asserted by him in accordance with sections 77 and 78 of the Copyright, Design and Patents Act 1988.

LIFE AT THE
EDGE

Free Run

STEPHEN RICHARD

Ransom

This is free running.

We are free runners.

In free running we try to get from one place to another place in a direct way.

Or across.

Free running started in France.

In France it's called *parkour*.

That's a French word. You say it like 'park – or'.

It means *course*, or *route*.

We want it to look like an art.

Making it look smooth and easy is a big part of free running.

For this reason we need to be strong.

We must trust our bodies.

We need a strong mind, too.

We must focus. All the time.

One slip and we could get hurt. Badly hurt.

We try to make it look easy.

But it isn't. We must train hard.

We never do anything reckless.

We make sure we are always as safe as we can be.

Don't just try it: that's too risky. You **will** get hurt.

You must learn how to land, so that when you jump, you don't get hurt.

You must learn good balance.

Free runners can run anywhere.

We don't need special clothes or equipment.

We need only good shoes with a grip, and loose clothes.

So it's cheap.

Anybody can try it.

Want to try free running?

Go to *www.parkourgenerations.com* to see how to get started.

Work with
Parkour Generations